C000127789

Save Funeral Costs™

2nd Edition

SW Barratt

savefuneralcosts.co.uk

Index

Introduction from the author SW Barratt

Firstly, thank you for reading **Save Funeral Costs**™ (SFC).

I wrote the Save Funeral Costs guide to help others after a relative died and the funeral had to be arranged. I visited the same undertaker that my family had used for over thirty years. They had always provided a good service which was not overly expensive in the past. As usual, the undertaker went through all the details and lastly told me the cost. I was shocked at how costs had risen for a basic cremation with one hearse, a limousine and a simple coffin. After registering the death and making inquiries, I found a low-cost undertaker who could offer cheaper funerals. The undertaker said the cost would be around half of the same funeral service I had been quoted two days before.

As most people would be, I was wary of why this was such a massive money-saving for the same service. It sounded too good to be true, yes, I would like to save money, but likewise did not want a poor-quality cheap funeral. The answer was reassuringly simple; the company I telephoned was a low-cost independent undertaker, sometimes known as an online undertaker. However, importantly they also promote budget funerals which are dignified cheaper funerals.

Since the first book was published, I have made continual improvements to the website and book. The main aim of SFC is to raise awareness that low-cost dignified funerals can easily be arranged, and for SFC to be an easy under one umbrella centre for all lower cost funeral help.

SW Barratt explains

Most people have not heard of independent low-cost undertakers due to powerful marketing domination from the few large national companies. These smaller low-cost undertakers cannot compete with the large marketing budgets of these companies.

About Save Funeral Costs

For cheaper funerals

Savings around 50%* can be made from many funeral charges.

Save Funeral Costs **savefuneralcosts.co.uk** (SFC) is an online consumer help centre which provides guidance for individuals to organise cheaper funerals, mainly via low-cost undertakers. SFC also explains where to find financial help, bereavement support, and advice on home and natural burials. The home page explains how SFC can help and directs the reader to low-cost undertakers and other money-saving information via the drop-down menus and grid boxes. These drop-down menus are also on each page.

Searches for cheaper funerals

Search terms such as, 'cheaper funerals' and 'low-cost funerals near me' are searched online terms, as many people struggle to finance a funeral. Whilst a lot of information is available, it can be confusing when searching from one source to another, as to who is low-cost. Save Funeral Costs aims to keep information together, and act as an accurate hub of support.

SFC books

The Save Funeral Costs eBook and paperback were published in 2020 by SW Barratt to assist the public in saving money on funeral costs. The book is written on SW's personal experience in arranging several family funerals. The goal of the book is to inform the reader of low-cost funeral directors and cost-saving funeral information. The book provides resources to inform individuals about saving significant money on funeral expenses.

In 2022, the second edition of the Save Funeral Costs guide was released, providing updated information and expanded resources for those looking to plan affordable funerals. The website also received an update to include more details on certain free financial assistance available from Government, charities, and other relevant services, that could be useful to individuals needing help planning a funeral.

SFC online

The book contents were used free of charge to populate the SFC website in 2021. The website's home page introduces the reader to low-cost undertakers and other money-saving information via the video, drop-down menus and grid boxes.

Objective

There is a common misunderstanding that unless you spend a lot of money, you are not able to give the deceased a decent funeral. Therefore, cheaper funerals would be out of the question for most people. The SFC objective is to explain that this is not the case, and aims to inform the reader of quality like-for-like services which cost much less.

It also aims to help those who either wish to save money, personalise a funeral, or are on a tight budget. Substantial money on funeral expenses can be saved by using all the relevant money-saving information in the one easy-to-read area.

Main content

SFC has several main areas that aim to assist the public in organising a cheaper funeral.

- Help with Funeral Costs
- Support with Bereavement
- Death Certificates
- Funeral Disbursements
- Cremations & Burials
- Funeral Packages
- Funeral Plans
- Writing a Will

- Funeral Directory

Steps 1-5 outline the main actions to be taken to reduce expenses.

- Step 1 Low-Cost Funerals
- Step 2 Funeral Service
- Step 3 Coffins Prices
- Step 4 Funeral Wake Ideas
- Step 5 Home & Natural Burial

The Directory page provides a comprehensive list of contact information for various funeral service providers and suppliers.

SFC is independent

SFC is not like many sites which are funded by sponsorship, subscription or general advertising. Neither is SFC like many other commercial sites which would prioritise or only promote services that pay them.

Everything written on SFC is independent and free from outside influence. This is to help the user access low-cost information free of charge. This is particularly important as some users would not be able to afford to pay.

SFC is run and founded by Steven W Barratt who employs various freelancers to carry out technical tasks such as site maintenance, graphic design and dealing with software issues.

SFC only earns an income if a user purchases from an affiliate link to a recommended product or service. This is at no extra expense to the user. If a company offers the best product or service but no affiliate link, they are still used to provide the user with the best deal.

Ongoing updates

Save Funeral Costs is designed to help the reader. The website has therefore undergone a series of updates since 2021, which involved the addition of weekly blog posts addressing different topics where readers may require advice. These blogs are also regularly featured on other popular social media platforms, including Quora, Medium, Facebook, LinkedIn, Instagram and Twitter.

In 2022, the website also introduced an opt-in email sign-up feature to allow readers to receive weekly blog posts which provides additional information and support to those seeking advice on reducing funeral costs. Both the SFC eBook and printed book had additional content added in 2023 and 2024 to include the updated website content.

Free PDF download & logo

In 2022, Save Funeral Costs released a Free Downloadable PDF "How to Save Funeral on Costs," a quick reference guide that includes the primary points from the book and website which include the Government Funeral Expenses Payment. **www.gov.uk/funeral-payments** The company logo was also registered in 2022.

Additional influence

Save Funeral Costs was additionally inspired by the 2018 Competition and Markets Authority (CMA) **www.gov.uk/cma-cases/funerals-market-study#final- report-and-decision-on-a-market-investigation-reference** findings which revealed that people were complaining about above-average inflation price rise and struggling to pay funeral bills, leading to debt. MP Frank Field **https://en.wikipedia.org/wiki/Frank_Field%_2C_Baron_Field_of_Birkenhead** welcomed the investigation and highlighted issues within the unregulated funeral industry. The CMA ordered undertakers and crematoriums to make their prices clear in 2021.

Down to Earth funeral advice operated by Quaker Social Action **www.quakersocialaction.org.uk/we-can-help/helping-funerals/down-earth** provided some information for the CMA investigation. The SunLife Cost of Dying 2023 Report **www.sunlife.co.uk/siteassets/documents/cost-of-dying/sunlife-cost-of-dying-report-2023.pdf** also highlighted that approximately 1 in 5 families had difficulty paying for a funeral, with around 1 in 7 families falling into debt.

One of the main reasons that low-cost undertakers can offer cheaper funerals than most other undertakers is that various other undertakers are owned by one of the few large national companies. In most cases, the name of the undertakers is on the shop front, but they are not independent. For example, a family business of J Smith & Son undertakers may have been in business for many years and then bought out by one of the large nationals but trade as J Smith & Son undertaker. Many people are often unaware that their local undertaker has been taken over until they receive correspondence for a funeral.

As most people are aware, once a large company starts to take control of smaller independents, costs can increase.

For further helpful information covering most aspects of cheaper funerals from lower cost headstones, poems, flowers, bereavement gift ideas, what to wear at a funeral, and much more, visit the Save Funeral Costs™ blog. **savefuneralcosts.co.uk/save-funeral-costs-blog**

* Save around 50% based on SunLife Cost of Dying 2023 report, which states the average cost of a basic cremation was £3673 in 2022. Low-cost TDM Funeral Services Simple Service £1941, this is a 47% difference.

Steps 1- 5

Steps 1 to 5 help save money, personalise and explain the various different funeral options. The quickest, simplest cost-saving method is to use Step 1 Low-Cost Undertakers. However, if you are able to put in a little more time, you could save more money on Step 2 Funeral Service, Step 3 Coffin Prices, and Step 4 Funeral Wake Ideas.

Alternatively, you may wish to use your local undertaker that you may have used in the past, but wish to personalise the funeral. You could save costs again, following Steps 2, 3, and 4.

Further savings may also be made from some Disbursements and Cremations and Burials. Any saved monies could then possibly be for a memorial service. Home & Natural Burial is covered in Step 5.

Please note:

All information and any costs are correct on publishing.

Please telephone or visit the links to confirm up to date information and costs.

1. Low-Cost Funerals

What are low-cost funerals?

Funerals can be expensive, but there are ways to reduce costs without sacrificing quality. One of the most effective ways to save on funeral expenses is by using a low-cost undertaker. Low-cost funerals are more affordable funeral services from low-cost undertakers, including direct cremation and burial without compromising on quality or dignity. By choosing a low-cost undertaker, you can save around 50%* on the cost of a traditional funeral.

How to find low-cost funerals

If searching for 'low-cost funerals near me', it's important to obtain a written scale of costs. This will help you compare prices and ensure you get the best deal. Listed below are low-cost undertakers, and the areas they cover.

TDM Funeral Services

www.tdmfunerals.co.uk South East England/ Nationwide for cremations and burials.

BB Funerals

www.brooks-funerals-directors.co.uk South East England and nationwide for cremations and burials.

The Funeral Market

www.thefuneralmarket.com for direct cremation and other attended cremation services covering all of the UK and most islands (excluding Northern Ireland).

Farewill

www.farewill.com for a direct cremation service covering all of the UK (excluding Northern Ireland).

Mitchells Funerals

www.mitchellsfunerals.co.uk for direct cremation, cremations, and burials covering southern Scotland – free funeral for 17 years and under.

Cremation Funeral

www.cremationfuneral.co.uk for a direct cremation in England and Wales.

Legacy Funerals

www.legacyfuneraldirectors.co.uk for direct cremation, cremations, and burials covering Hull and East Yorkshire.

Caledonia Cremation

www.caledoniacremation.org.uk for a direct cremation covering mainland Scotland.

Pure Cremation

https://ni.purecremation.com for a direct cremation covering Northern Ireland.

A direct cremation funeral

A direct cremation is sometimes referred to as a cheap cremation funeral or cheap funeral. Importantly this does not mean that you will have a cheap funeral service, you will receive a fully dignified service at a low-cost.

Direct cremation is one of the most affordable cremation funeral options available. This type of funeral involves the collection of the deceased and later taken to the crematorium in a simple coffin. You can choose to have the ashes delivered to you or scattered Additional services such as a doctor's certificate and having the ashes returned can be an extra cost.

If you're interested in saving even more money, consider arranging the funeral service yourself. You can inform the undertaker that you will arrange for someone to carry out the service and that you will be supplying the coffin. However, if you have arranged a direct cremation or package, you may not be able to change the coffin.

An affordable funeral

In addition to choosing a low-cost undertaker, there are other ways to have an affordable funeral. For example, you could ask your guests to make their way to the crematorium or cemetery instead of hiring a limousine for close family and friends. This would mean that just a hearse is needed to transport the coffin.

All undertakers, whether independent or not, can arrange a spokesperson to carry out the service so that you do not have to. Although it will save you money if you were to directly book the spokesperson, details are in Step 2.

Searching for the cheapest funeral

When searching it is not always clear who are low-cost undertakers, who can provide the cheapest funeral.

Searching is often time-consuming and inaccurate. For these reasons and to help the reader, low-cost undertaker services are listed to avoid confusion.

A wake is not quoted as standard costs from undertakers, as not all mourners would like one.

At this stage, when it comes to saving expenses, if you only use a low- cost undertaker and nothing more listed in the book, you would have already saved a large amount of money.

If, however, you wish to save more money and put in a little more time you could look into Steps 2, 3 and 4. These are informing the undertaker that you will arrange someone to carry out the service, that you will be supplying the coffin and organising the reception. If you have booked a direct cremation or package, then you may not be able to change the coffin.

Disbursements vary from different undertakers, so it is always best to get an emailed or written scale of costs.

Summary

When making inquiries, it's advisable to ask for a written scale of costs. You can then be clear about the final amount if shopping around for the cheapest funeral cost. It can also save unnecessary telephone calls to the undertaker if you forget to ask or write something down when speaking to them.

Combining a low-cost undertaker and direct cremation is the best way of arranging a cheaper funeral.

* Save around 50% based on the SunLife Cost of Dying 2023 Report, which states the average cost of a basic cremation was

£3,673 in 2022. Low-cost TDM Funeral Services Simple Service £1941. This is a 47% difference.

2. Funeral Service

When it comes to booking a spokesperson to read the funeral service many people are unaware that it will save them money to pay a spokesperson or religious person of their faith directly and not through the undertaker.

Why have a service?

The service is an important aspect of saying goodbye to a loved one who has passed away. It involves a speech or speeches that honours the life of the deceased and provides closure to family and friends.

Religious funeral service

To book a religious spokesperson, ask the undertaker who they use for cremation or burial service; then go directly to that person. Alternatively, visit your church/place of worship and ask if a religious person can conduct the service.

You could use the Salvation Army which normally asks for a donation. Contact details for the Salvation Army are on page 93.

Non-religious funeral service

If you prefer a non-religious funeral service, you could use a Humanist. Humanists throughout the UK can be contacted directly through the British Humanist Association. They can also offer religious activities such as a hymn or music of praise, provided there is no act of worship. Contact details for Humanists are on page 93.

Similarly, Celebrants offer non-religious services that can also include religious acts in the service. By booking a Celebrant or Humanist directly, you can save on funeral expenses. Contact details for Celebrants are on page 93.

Funeral order of service

The order of service typically includes several standard elements to guide the mourners and person reading the service, such as:

- <u>Introduction</u> This may include a welcome message from the spokesperson or a brief statement about the purpose and significance of the service.
- <u>Hymns or music</u> This section lists the hymns, songs, or instrumental music that will be played during the service.
- <u>Prayers or readings</u> This section includes any prayers, readings, or poems that will be recited during the service. It may also include personal tributes from family members or friends.
- <u>Committal</u> This section typically includes the final words of farewell and any final blessings or prayers.
- <u>Closing</u> This section may include a final hymn or song, as well as information about any post-funeral gatherings or events.

The exact format and content of the order of service can vary depending on the cultural and religious traditions of the deceased and their family, as well as personal preferences and requests. It is often created in collaboration with the funeral director, the officiant or clergy member, and the family members of the deceased.

Cost-saving tips

A funeral service can be expensive, but there are ways to save money without compromising on the quality of the service. One of the ways is to book the spokesperson directly. You could also create and print your own funeral service order, as this would obviously save paying an undertaker.

Direct cremation or burial skips the service and allows you to have a private memorial service with close family and friends. Another cost-saving tip is to opt for a simple coffin or cremation urn instead of an expensive one.

Planning the service

Planning a funeral service can be overwhelming, especially if you are grieving. Here are some steps to help you plan a funeral service:

- Choose the type of service you want
- Decide on the venue, date, and time of the service
- Choose the music and readings for the service
- Decide who will deliver the eulogy
- Decide on the type of flowers or donations
- Choose the pallbearers and ushers for the service
- Decide on the transportation to the service
- Choose the type of burial or cremation you want

Summary

By booking a spokesperson directly you are again saving funeral expenses, and working towards an affordable funeral. You will often find that home visits are available from each of the above service providers.

A funeral service is an important part of saying goodbye to a loved one. By understanding the types of services available, cost-saving tips, and how to plan a funeral service, you can make informed decisions that honour the life of the deceased and provide closure to family and friends.

3. Coffin Prices

When it comes to planning a funeral, one of the significant costs can be the coffin. Coffin prices in the UK can vary widely depending on the type of coffin you choose. Many different types of coffin and links to their costs are listed to help find the cheapest coffin prices. Coffins for cremation such as cardboard use less energy to burn than traditional wood. Cardboard, wooden and wicker coffin prices are the most commonly searched for, lead lined coffin prices being less popular.

Coffin prices in the UK vary widely depending on the type of coffin you choose. You can buy coffins from suppliers who deliver throughout the UK which are shown below. However, in some cases you will only be able to buy through an undertaker. For up-to-date prices on a chosen coffin visit the links below.

- Willow **www.sussexwillowcoffins.co.uk**
- Wicker **www.somersetwillowcoffins.co.uk**
- Timber **www.feetfirstcoffins.co.uk**
- Cardboard **www.cardboardcoffincompany.com**
- Banana leaves **www.naturalwovencoffins.co.uk/ products/coffins/banana-leaf-coffins** Not supplied to the public – purchase from funeral director
- Pandanus leaves **www.thegreencoffincompany.co.uk/ pandanus-round-ended-coffin**
- Cane **www.naturalwovencoffins.co.uk/products/ coffins/cane-coffins/** Not supplied to the public – purchase from funeral director
- Seagrass **www.naturalwovencoffins.co.uk/products/ coffins/seagrass-coffins** Not supplied to the public – purchase from funeral director
- Bamboo **www.thegreencoffincompany.co.uk/ bamboo-coffins**
- Wool **www.awhainsworth.co.uk/our-brands/ natural-legacy** Not supplied to the public – ask your funeral director to purchase through JC Atkinson Tel: 0191 415 1516

Types of coffins

There are many different types of coffins available, including cardboard and chipboard. Eco-friendly options made from natural timber, bamboo, banana leaves, cane, pandanus leaves, seagrass, willow, and wool. Each type of coffin has its own unique features and benefits to the person purchasing it.

Natural timber coffins

Image copyright and courtesy of Feet First Coffins

Environmentally friendly timber coffins are perhaps the most traditional of coffins. However, it's important to check that the timber is sourced from sustainable sources. It is important not to contribute to deforestation or a loss of natural habitat. Most natural timber coffins are joined together with wooden dowels not metal screws or nails. This is so that there are non-biodegradable items in the coffin. Handles are normally natural rope, which again degradable. These handmade coffins are not the lowest coffin prices due to the labour in making them.

Cardboard coffins

Cardboard coffins take around 60% less energy to burn with up to 90% less emissions compared to wood. It is for these reasons that some people prefer cardboard coffins for cremations.

Cardboard coffins are made from recycled cardboard and are designed to be biodegradable, making them a popular choice for people who are looking for a sustainable and affordable option for their loved one's final resting place.

One of the main benefits of cardboard coffins is their affordability. They are typically much less expensive than traditional coffins made from wood, metal, or other materials. This can be a particularly important consideration for people who are on a budget or who want to keep coffin prices as low as possible.

Another benefit of cardboard coffins is their sustainability. Because they are made from recycled materials, they have a low environmental impact. They are also designed to biodegrade quickly and safely, without releasing harmful chemicals or gases into the environment.

Cardboard coffins are also customisable, with many companies offering the option to personalise the coffin with artwork, photographs, or messages. This can make them a meaningful and personal choice for those who are looking for a way to honour their loved one's memory.

I once attended a funeral where the family had purchased a cardboard coffin online, had it delivered to their home and the children painted the coffin in bright colours and flowers. The undertaker then picked the coffin up from the family. Interestingly, this was not to save money. The family wanted a more environmentally friendly coffin and asked the children to paint the coffin so that the funeral would not be so sombre. It all worked very well.

If you were planning to decorate the coffin, then you are often told to use water-based paints, such as emulsion, powder paint or acrylics. Cardboard coffins can come as a plain brown colour or white finish.

Chipboard coffins

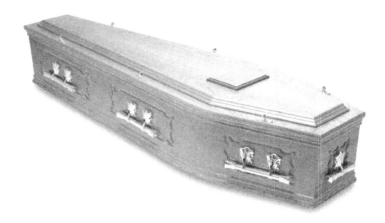

Chipboard coffins, also known as particle board coffins, are an affordable option for funerals. These coffins are made from recycled wood chips that are compressed and bonded together with a resin adhesive to create a strong and durable material.

The surface is then usually covered in a thin plastic veneer to imitate a wood grain look.

One of the main benefits of chipboard coffins is their affordability. They are typically much less expensive than traditional coffins made from wood, metal, or other materials. This can be a particularly important consideration for people who are on a budget or who want to keep funeral expenses and coffin prices as low as possible.

Chipboard coffins are also customisable, with many companies offering the option to personalise the coffin with artwork, photographs, or messages. This can make them a meaningful and personal choice for those who are looking for a way to honour their loved one's memory.

In addition, chipboard coffins are often designed to look similar to traditional coffins, so they can be a good option for people who want a more traditional appearance without the high cost.

Chipboard coffins are sometimes referred to as a traditional veneered coffin. Apparently, around 80% of coffins used for burial are chipboard construction. They are the most popular choice due to their affordability and ease of manufacture.

Due to the resins used to bond the chipboard together these coffins are not environmentally friendly as they emit toxins into the earth for over 100 years. They will in time completely decay provided no plastic or metal handles are fitted.

Wicker coffins

Wicker coffins, also known as willow coffins, are an Eco-friendly and sustainable option for funerals in the UK. These coffins are made from woven willow or other natural materials, making them a popular choice for people who want to honour the deceased in a way that is environmentally friendly.

One of the main benefits of wicker coffins is their Eco-friendliness. They are made from renewable and biodegradable materials, which means they have a low environmental impact. They are also designed to biodegrade quickly and safely, without releasing harmful chemicals or gases into the environment.

Another benefit of wicker coffins is their natural appearance. They are often handcrafted and can be customised with personal touches, such as flowers or ribbons. This can make them a meaningful and personal choice.

Wicker coffins are also a lightweight option, which can make them easier to transport and handle during the funeral service. They are also typically less expensive than traditional coffins made from wood, metal, or other materials, making them a good option for those on a budget.

Eco-coffins

Eco-friendly coffins are a growing trend in the UK as people become increasingly concerned about the impact of traditional burial practices on the environment. These coffins are made from sustainable materials such as some of those listed. They are designed to biodegrade quickly and naturally. Cardboard coffins without the waterproof liner are also classed as Eco-friendly coffins.

One of the main benefits of Eco-friendly coffins is their reduced environmental impact. Traditional coffins are typically made from materials such as hardwood, or chipboard which can take decades or even centuries to break down in the earth. This can lead to the release of harmful chemicals and greenhouse gases into the environment. Eco-friendly coffins, on the other hand, are made from natural materials that break down quickly and safely, without harming the environment.

Another benefit of Eco-friendly coffins is their affordability. Traditional coffins can be expensive, with some costing thousands of pounds. Eco-friendly coffins, on the other hand, are often much more affordable, making them a good option for people who want to reduce their environmental impact without breaking the bank.

Eco-friendly coffins are also often seen as a more personal and meaningful choice. Traditional coffins can feel impersonal and sterile, but Eco-friendly coffins are often more rustic and natural-looking, which can be more fitting for someone who had a strong connection to nature.

Lead-lined coffins

Some traditional solid wood coffins can be lead lined, although this is not normally required unless transporting a body overseas. However, the use of lead-lined coffins is becoming less common due to environmental concerns. Lead is a toxic substance and can poison the soil, potentially contaminating groundwater and other natural resources. As a result, many countries have implemented regulations to limit the use of lead in coffins, or have banned it altogether.

Coffins for cremation

Cardboard coffins are becoming increasingly popular due to their Eco-friendly nature. They take around 60% less energy to burn compared to wood, and emit up to 90% fewer emissions.

If you're purchasing a coffin for cremation, it is crucial to ensure with the manufacturer that it is FFMA (Funeral Furnishing Manufacturers' Association) approved. **www.ffma.co.uk/ test-protocol** approved. This means that it is a suitable coffin for cremation as it conforms to regulations.

Coffins with an FFMA certificate are also recommended for burial, as they are lined and have a board in the base to give the coffin strength. This is especially important for wicker and cardboard coffins.

Natural burial sites

If you're planning a natural burial, it's important to keep in mind that embalming is not allowed due to the chemicals used. Similarly, cardboard coffins may not be accepted at natural burial sites due to the waterproofing chemical which is sometimes used to line the inside of them. To read more on

natural burials visit. **www.naturaldeath.org.uk/index.php?
page=natural-burial-grounds**

It is crucial to inquire about the type of coffin allowed before making a purchase.

Summary

Coffin prices in the UK can vary widely depending on the type of coffin you choose. It's important to keep in mind the different materials available, regulations to follow, and eco-friendly options. Choosing the right coffin can make a significant difference in the cost of a funeral, as well as its impact on the environment.

To read further about Eco-friendly coffins visit. **savefuneralcosts.co.uk/environmentally-friendly-coffins-are-they-possible**. To paint and personalise a coffin, you could have the coffin delivered to your home and later collected by the undertaker. If the undertaker cannot collect, there is a van transport service on page 96.

4. Funeral Wake Ideas

Losing a loved one is a difficult experience, and planning a funeral wake can be overwhelming. But with the right ideas and planning, you can create a unique and meaningful event that celebrates the life of your loved one. For many having a funeral wake at home is often the simplest wake to organise.

Why have a wake?

A funeral wake is a gathering of friends and family after a funeral service to offer condolences, share memories of the deceased and support each other during a difficult time. While funeral customs vary around the world, the funeral wake is a longstanding tradition in England and has many benefits.

Firstly, a funeral wake provides an opportunity for people to come together and offer support to each other. Losing a loved one can be a deeply emotional and isolating experience, but being surrounded by friends and family can provide a sense of comfort and connection. The wake allows people to share their grief, reminisce about the deceased and offer each other words of encouragement.

Secondly, a funeral wake provides an opportunity to celebrate the life of the deceased. While a funeral service is often a sombre occasion, a wake can be a more relaxed and informal event. People can share stories and memories of the deceased, toast to their life, and celebrate the positive impact they had on those around them. This celebration of life can be a healing experience for those in mourning and can help them to focus on the positive aspects of their loved one's life.

Thirdly, a funeral wake can help to create a sense of closure. After a funeral service, people often feel a sense of disorientation or detachment from reality. Attending a wake can help to ground people, allowing them to acknowledge the reality of the situation and start to process their grief. By spending time with others who are going through a similar experience, people can feel less alone and more prepared to move forward.

Fourthly, a funeral wake can help to preserve the memory of the deceased. By sharing stories and memories, people can keep the memory of the deceased alive and ensure that they are not forgotten. This can be especially important for people who were not able to attend the funeral service or for those who want to continue to honour the memory of their loved one in the months and years to come.

Finally, a funeral wake can help to strengthen social bonds. In today's fast-paced and often isolated society, it can be difficult to maintain close relationships with friends and family. The wake provides an opportunity to reconnect with people and strengthen social bonds. This can be particularly important for people who live far away or who have lost touch with family members.

Do you have to have a wake after a funeral?

This is a commonly asked question, but there is no requirement to hold a wake after the funeral, it is personal choice, and the wish of the deceased.

Why is a wake called a wake?

The word "wake" originates from the Old English word "wacian," which means "to watch" or "to be awake." In medieval times, it was customary for family and friends to keep watch over a deceased person's body overnight, as a way of showing respect and guarding against evil spirits. This practice became known as "sitting up with the dead" or simply "the wake." Over the years, the term modern use of the word wake has come to refer not just to the vigil itself, but to the remembrance that follows a person's death.

Hosting a funeral wake: Do it yourself or hire a venue?

In most cases, booking a venue directly is more cost-effective than going through an undertaker or booking agent. However, if you're looking to save even more money, you could consider having the funeral wake at home and preparing the food yourself.

While this option can be quite a bit of work, it can also be more personal and meaningful. However, as this is quite a fair amount of work at an emotional time it may not be suitable for many people.

Church receptions: An affordable option

If you're looking for an affordable venue to host a funeral wake, consider checking with your local church. Some church halls offer low-cost rentals for a few hours, making them a budget-friendly option. However, keep in mind that you will need to supply the food and drinks, or hire a catering firm, which may not be suitable for everyone. You can also look in local directories and online for function rooms, hall hire, and church halls to hire near to you.

Public Houses: A relaxed atmosphere

Another option for hosting a funeral wake is at a local public house (Pub). This venue can be easier to arrange and often has a relaxed and friendly atmosphere. Many pubs have a private area that can be reserved for mourners, and they can often supply the food. Guests can purchase their drinks, so there is no financial pressure on the family to cover the drinks bill.

Families who do not want the reception to be dreary will often find a brighter atmosphere in the pub. These brighter receptions are often lower in cost compared to hiring halls and catering firms.

Personalise the event with unique touches

No matter where you choose to host the wake, you can add unique touches to personalise the event. For example, you could create a photo collage or display of your loved one's favourite things. You could also incorporate their favourite foods or drinks into the menu.

Another option is to have a memory table where guests can write down their favourite memories of your loved one.

Other funeral wake ideas

If you're looking for more funeral wake ideas, here are a few other options to consider:

- Outdoor picnic If your loved one enjoyed spending time outdoors, consider hosting an outdoor picnic. You could choose a park or other outdoor location and ask guests to bring their own food and drinks.
- Balloon release A balloon release is a beautiful way to honour your loved one. You could choose a favourite

colour or theme and have guests release the balloons together.

- <u>Candle lighting ceremony</u> A candle lighting ceremony is a touching way to remember your loved one. You could provide candles for guests to light in memory of your loved one.
- <u>Videos</u> Video montage of the deceased is often an engaging way to celebrate their life.
- <u>Bingo</u> If the deceased was a keen player, you could organise a short fun game of bingo.
- <u>Decorate the venue</u> Images of the deceased pinned around the venue and personal possessions are often a good idea to display.
- <u>Mourner involvement</u> Sometimes mourners would like to say a few words about the life of the deceased.

Summary

Planning a funeral wake can be a challenging task, but with the right ideas and planning, you can create a unique and memorable event that celebrates the life of your loved one. Whether you choose to host the wake at a venue or at home, remember that adding personal touches can make all the difference.

To read more on funeral wake ideas visit.
savefuneralcosts.co.uk/funeral-wakes

5. Home & Natural Burial

Natural burial, also known as woodland burial, is an alternative funeral method that is gaining popularity in the UK. Listed below are the benefits of natural burials. Home deaths, hospital deaths, and home garden burials are also explained.

Home deaths

As there is no legal requirement to use an undertaker, you can carry out all of the funeral arrangements once you have registered the death, have the death certificate, and any other paperwork. This is probably the most cost-saving method, often referred to as a do-it-yourself funeral, or the cheapest possible funeral. In practice, not many people want to, or be able to get involved in carrying out a funeral at home or transporting a body to the cemetery, crematorium or burial ground.

If the death is at home and a post-mortem is not required, you can store the body at home; however, this is generally for a week maximum and in a cool area. A week is not long, and in more built-up residential areas or over Christmas or bank holidays it may not be possible to arrange and have the funeral within a week. If the deceased had bedsores, ulcers, infections, or other conditions that could accelerate decomposition, it's best to store the body at a local undertaker's refrigerated storage. If a post-mortem is required, the hospital will store the body for you until you are ready to collect it.

Hospital deaths

When a death occurs in a hospital, the hospital will usually store the body for a reasonable period in refrigerated storage while you arrange the funeral. You can collect the body from the hospital if you have appropriate transportation or hire a vehicle. The mortuary staff can sometimes dress the deceased in the clothes of your choice and place the body in the coffin.

Normally you would collect the deceased the night before or in the morning of the funeral if there is time. You can, of course, also take the coffin straight to the crematorium; the staff can then take the coffin for cremation.

Home garden burials

If you want to save on burial costs, you could arrange a home garden burial. However, you must comply with relevant regulations, such as obtaining necessary permissions from local authorities **www.gov.uk/find-local-council** and ensuring that the burial site meets groundwater regulations.

For example, you may need various permission/s as your garden may then be classed as a burial site. There are also regulations not to contaminate groundwater by not burying the body within a certain distance of running/standing water, field drains, ditches, a well, borehole or spring etc. It's best to check with the Environment Agency **www.gov.uk/ government/organisations/environment-agency** for groundwater regulations, including how deep the grave must be. Contact details for the Environment Agency are on page 97.

You do not have to purchase a coffin, but you will need to keep a record of the grave and update the property deeds. Digging a grave can be dangerous, so you may wish to hire a professional grave digging service. Contact details for a grave digging service are on page 97.

The benefits of natural burial

The Natural Death Centre **www.naturaldeath.org.uk/ index.php?page=natural-burial-grounds** can inform you of natural burial grounds in the UK, which can offer a rural, often very peaceful location. Contact details for the Natural Death Centre are on page 96.

These natural burial sites offer several benefits, including cost savings, environmental advantages, and a peaceful, rural location. Unfortunately, natural burial sites do not accept embalmed bodies due to the toxic chemicals used in the embalming process.

Cost-savings

Natural burial is often the most cost-effective option for a funeral. Since you can carry out all the arrangements yourself, you can save on fees charged by undertakers. Additionally, woodland burial plots tend to be less expensive than traditional burial plots in cities.

Environmental advantages

Natural burial is also a more environmentally friendly option. Instead of using toxic chemicals in the embalming process and non-biodegradable coffins, natural burial sites encourage the use of biodegradable coffins, shrouds, or blankets, and prohibit the use of embalming fluids. There are other environmental advantages such as not leaving a carbon footprint created from a headstone manufacturer.

This option involves burying the body in a biodegradable casket or shroud in a natural setting, allowing the body to decompose naturally and become part of the ecosystem.

Natural burials are gaining in popularity as people become more conscious of their impact on the environment and seek more sustainable and meaningful ways to say goodbye to their loved ones.

It must be remembered that there are no headstones allowed in natural/woodland burial sites.

Woodland burials

Natural woodland burial sites are often located in rural areas and offer a serene, peaceful environment for burial. Many people find this setting to be more comforting and fitting for their loved ones.

General information

If you're planning a crematorium service, and then bury the urn of ashes you may need coffin bearers to walk with and place the coffin in the chapel of rest. Inform the crematorium that you are conducting the funeral and not an undertaker. Certain items cannot be placed in a coffin as they could damage the cremator. Contact details for handmade urns are on page 96.

For example, pacemakers can explode and blast a hole in the wall of the cremator; glass objects can also explode. You would need to pay an undertaker to remove a pacemaker or anything else that could damage the cremator. A morning cremation may save you costs compared to later in the day.

Cemetery burial plots can alter enormously in cost, rural burial plots are generally cheaper than city ones. Discounts are usually made for burials within the same borough where the deceased lived.

Contrary to a lot of belief, you do not have to embalm the body of someone who has died from cancer. Local funeral directors can inform you about their fees and storage facilities.

Summary

Home burials are the cheapest and the most personal burial, but it can put certain amendments on the property deeds and possibly de-value the property. Natural and woodland burials offer an environmentally friendly burial solution at a low-cost.

However, embalmed bodies and headstones are not allowed. A lack of headstone may not be suitable for many who would like to visit the grave. Likewise, the lack of a headstone would make it difficult explaining to others where the grave is.

To read more about natural burials visit.
savefuneralcosts.co.uk/discover-natural-burials/

Help with Funeral Costs

Free† Financial Help

What happens if you cannot afford to pay for a funeral?

Firstly, check to see if there is any help with funeral costs by looking to see if the deceased had life insurance. A policy can either pay for or help towards the costs. There may be property to sell, or savings, in which case you should contact a solicitor and ask if any savings can be released to pay the funeral bill before the sale of the property and possible probate process.

The Government paid out the substantial sum of £62.5 million in 2020-2021 from their Funeral Expenses Payment (FEP) scheme. FEP is under **Government help with funeral costs**.

You could ask any other relatives if they can contribute. You should also inquire with your local social security office or online to see if you are entitled to financial help towards funeral costs.

What is a Paupers Funeral?

If nobody has any money, the family is unwilling to pay an undertaker, and there is no other help with funeral costs from the Government then ask your local council or hospital for a public health funeral. This used to be called a 'Paupers Funeral'.

Death from a crime

If the deceased has died from a crime, you may be able to claim compensation. You usually have to file a claim within two years of the crime. Additionally, the crime; should have been reported to the police before applying. If in doubt, always check with either the police or a solicitor.

Possible charity help

Turn2us
https://grants-search.turn2us.org.uk charity may be able to help you with a funeral grant.
Freephone: 0808 802 2000

Child Funeral Charity
www.childfuneralcharity.org.uk can help with costs not covered by the Children's Funeral Fund.
Tel: 01480 276088

Friends of the Elderly
www.fote.org.uk help with costs not covered by Government help. You have to be aged 66 or over to claim, and the claim has to be through a professional person or organisation such as the Citizens Advice Bureau. Although the claimant has to be aged 66 or over, the deceased can be any age.
Tel: 0207 730 8263

Money Helper

For informative advice on financial help if not receiving Government benefits.

www.moneyhelper.org.uk/en/family-and-care/death-and-bereavement/help-paying-for-a-funeral?source=mas

Terminal illness benefits

Advice from Marie Curie

www.mariecurie.org.uk/help/support/benefits-entitlements/benefits-social-care-system/what-benefits-can-i-claim#what
Freephone: 0800 090 2309

a) Government help with funeral costs

If you receive certain benefits, then you may be entitled to:

England and Wales: Funeral Expenses Payment
www.gov.uk/funeral-payments
Freephone: 0800 151 2012

Scotland: Funeral Support Payment
www.mygov.scot/funeral-support-payment/if-the-person-who-died-was-18-or-over
Freephone: 0800 731 0469

Northern Ireland: Funeral Expenses Payment
www.nidirect.gov.uk/articles/funeral-expenses-payments
Freephone: 0800 085 2463

b) Government help with children's funeral costs

England: Children's Funeral Fund
www.gov.uk/child-funeral-costs
Freephone: 0808 196 1759

Wales: Funeral Contribution
https://gov.wales/child-funeral-and-other-related-costs-information-html
Tel: 0300 060 4400
There are no cremation or burial fees for children under 18 in Wales. The contribution can help additional costs.

England, Wales and Northern Ireland: Funeral Expenses Payment
www.gov.uk/funeral-payments
You may also be entitled to this payment if you receive certain benefits.
Freephone: 0800 151 2012

Scotland: Funeral Support Payment
www.mygov.scot/funeral-support-payment/if-the-person-who-died-was-17-or-under if you receive certain benefits.
Freephone: 0800 182 2222

There are no cremation or burial fees for children under 17 in Scotland. The payment can help additional costs.

Northern Ireland: The Child Funeral Fund
www.nidirect.gov.uk/articles/child-funeral-fund
Freephone: 0800 232 1271

Government Budgeting Loan

England/Wales/Scotland:
www.gov.uk/budgeting-help-benefits
Freephone: 0800 169 0140

Northern Ireland:
www.nidirect.gov.uk/articles/social-fund-budgeting-loan
Tel: 0800 022 4250

Save Funeral Costs does not encourage people to get into debt to pay for a funeral. However, there are often cases whereby an individual or family needs help with funeral costs and has to borrow money. In this situation, it is sensible to borrow the money interest-free from the Government instead of a bank or loan company.

The Budgeting Loan has replaced the Crisis Loan for funeral payments. Claimants must be in receipt of certain benefits to claim the interest-free loan. The loan is generally paid back from the claimant's monthly benefit payments. You can claim the loan as well as payments listed in **a)** & **b)** on page 43.

Government Bereavement Support Payment

England/Wales/Scotland/Northern Ireland:
www.gov.uk/bereavement-support-payment
Freephone: 0800 151 2012

Spouses or civil partners may be able to claim the bereavement support payment. It should be claimed within three months of the death, although it is still possible to claim up to twenty-one months, and in some cases beyond. This benefit was previously known as Widowed Parent's Allowance, Bereavement Allowance, and Bereavement Payment. It is available to those under the state pension age and provides financial help to people who have lost a spouse or civil partner on or after 6 April 2017.

Government probate information

General inquiries and to apply for Probate in England and Wales.
www.gov.uk/government/organisations/hm-revenue-customs/contact/probate-general-enquiries
Tel: 0300 123 1072

There are different probate rules in Scotland
www.scotcourts.gov.uk/taking-action/dealing-with-a-deceased%27s-estate-in-scotland where it is called Confirmation,

Tel: 0131 444 3300

and different probate rules in Northern Ireland.
www.nidirect.gov.uk/articles/probate
Tel: 0300 200 7812

In some cases, you may wish to stop a probate application
www.gov.uk/stop-probate-application
(lodge a caveat) due to legal reasons.
Tel: 0300 303 0648

Please refer to the above Scottish and Northern Ireland telephone numbers to lodge a caveat in these areas.

Low-cost probate services

Solicitors can charge a percentage between 2% and 5% of the estate value to carry out probate, which can obviously be a high fee. For example, if the estate is £500,000 there would be a £10,000 to £25,000 plus VAT- (£12,000 to £30,000) fee.

Thankfully, Farewill below offer a low fixed fee of £595.00 or from £1,500.00.

Many people find themselves needing probate to release monies from the estate. Generally, probate is required if more than £10,000 of assets are held by the deceased. Probate can take between one and three months to complete.

Ensure you have all the documents to hand before contacting the links below.

Farewill offer 'Essential Probate' from £595.00 (+ probate registry fee) for a basic service with a simple to-sort estate whereby you would fill out most of the paperwork. They also offer 'Complete Probate' from £1,500.00 for a full service if you are too busy and /or the estate is complex.

Farewill probate **www.farewill.com/apply-for-probate**
Tel: 0208 138 0719

† Free financial help applies if the claimant is in receipt of certain Government benefits or is eligible for charity help.

Support with Bereavement

Dealing with the loss of a loved one can be overwhelming. Many mourners experience the need for support with bereavement, and that people in their environment such as relatives, neighbours, and friends, have a hard time dealing with grief. Some evade, and others give advice. But this advice is sometimes more problematic than helpful to the mourners.

It is best to focus on the problem head-on and look at how to deal with it, as opposed to running away from it. People handle grief differently. Some people feel as if they will never get over the death. Whereas some people find that six months of mourning has healed them fully.

In one of the last phases, the mourner establishes a relationship with their surroundings and themselves. However, mourners can also slip back into a state of grief again. You can't put a time-frame on healing. Grief affects us all differently, and there are no set rules on how to deal with it. Many people reach out to professionals for support with bereavement, as they can try therapies that can assist. Memories will keep you from moving forwards more often than not. Bereavement support groups can also be very helpful, as you are mixing with other people in the same position.

During the phases of mourning, the order, intensity and duration are different for each person. Therefore, grief is individual and does not follow any scheme. Older models of the mourning phases stated that the task of the bereaved was to detach themselves from the deceased in order to progress on. Today we know that this contradicts the experience of most mourners. Most have a need to maintain a connection to the deceased in a different form.

Joining a bereavement support group can provide much-needed help and support during this emotional time.

Bereavement support groups

Bereavement support groups are a safe space where people who have lost loved ones can come together to share their experiences, thoughts and feelings. These groups provide emotional support, practical advice, and a sense of community.

They offer a way to connect with others who understand what you are going through.

If you are struggling with grief, it's important to seek help. Grief can cause depression and anxiety, and it can be challenging to deal with on your own. Support groups can help you deal with your emotions and provide a supportive community during this difficult time.

Understanding grief

Grief is a complex process that can be challenging to navigate. There are no set stages of grief, but there are some common emotions that people experience when dealing with loss:

- Consuming thoughts for the deceased
- Unable to enjoy good memories of the deceased
- Feeling sad, emotional, angry
- A loss of enthusiasm
- Unable to accept the death

In the beginning, there is often denial. They may be unable to somehow integrate the loss into life. In the second phase, strong emotions break through, often contradicting each other. It may be that anger sprouts up against the deceased, or past injuries all come back into thought. In the next moment, you feel deep anxiety and feel the connection, but realise this connection no longer exists in its original form.

There are many coping strategies that can help with grief. Some people find comfort in creating small routines, such as lighting a candle or visiting a loved one's grave. Others find solace in sports or exercise, which can help relieve tension and boost energy levels. Keeping a diary, organising daily tasks, and taking small steps can also be beneficial. All these actions on their own or collectively can be a form of support with bereavement.

It's essential to remember that grieving is a personal process, and you should take your time to find what works best for you. Grief affects everyone differently, and there is no right or wrong way to grieve.

You need to first understand grief to then be able to deal with it. According to many professional websites, grief needs space; the ways to create space are very different. Small routines, such as the picture of the deceased on the window sill, lighting a candle, and the walk to the grave, can all be important. Others listen to certain music, write a diary, and have special days out. Some ask themselves, what would be good for me? The pain can keep returning, and dealing with it actively can help.

Sports and exercise also help to relieve tension and feel vitality again; when you feel out of balance. You may feel you need a distraction, but also time to grieve. Crying is also good; it can provide support with bereavement as it purges many emotions and helps you make a clear connection between your pain and thinking straight.

Help with bereavement

There are many different types of help with bereavement available, including online groups, local community groups, and more structured therapy groups.

Professional support should be sought if the grief exclusively determines everyday life for a very long time and restricts it very strongly. There are many types of diagnoses for "persistent grief disorder" in psychotherapy. Therapists feel challenged here to find and determine the line between "normal" and "in need of treatment".

It is positive that this diagnosis means that grief is no longer classified and treated as depression because it is not. With depression, emotions are absent – with grief, they are strong. Getting bereavement and illness help can often be your first step in dealing with a situation. Grief can cause depression and anxiety, the Samaritans **www.samaritans.org** can offer help. You should reach out immediately if you feel you can't cope. Signs of depression include:

- Poor diet
- Lack of concentration
- Poor responses
- Feeling melancholy
- Bad decision making
- No energy for basic tasks
- Thoughts of dying

Dealing with grief is never easy, but joining a bereavement support group can provide the help and support you need in a safe and supportive environment where people can connect with others who understand what they are going through. Local hospitals and hospices have information on local groups. You can also search online for support groups that are specific to your type of loss.

A daily plan in which you take small steps will help you to organise at least the bare minimum. Keeping a diary can help, but staying organised with your own priorities will greatly assist you. Another thing to remember is that you are never alone. There are always people to help and others in the same situation.

It's important not to do anything out of character during this emotional time as you may regret it later. Quitting your job, selling your home or breaking up with a partner, these can be made in haste, which can be destructive long term.

Mesothelioma support

Abestos.com **www.asbestos.com** are USA leaders in Mesothelioma resources (cancer from asbestos).

The different bereavement support groups shown below are established organisations which are free to use.

For additional help the blog post entitled Bereavement Counselling Support **savefuneralcosts.co.uk/bereavement-counselling/** gives further guidance on support with bereavement.

Mesothelioma Hope
Mesothelioma Hope is an American based organisation that provides in-depth specialist help and advice on this rare fatal cancer. Caused from asbestos, this cancer forms in the lungs (Pleural Mesothelioma) or abdomen (Peritoneal Mesothelioma). They also offer advice on all aspects for people suffering from this terminal illness, including different treatments and drugs.
Visit: **www.mesotheliomahope.com**
Telephone: 001 855 722 2974

Marie Curie
Marie Curie provides practical information and support on all aspects of life with terminal illness, caring for someone and bereavement, over the phone, via web chat, online, in print, and through an online community.
Visit: **www.mariecurie.org.uk/help**
Freephone: 0800 090 2309

Down to Earth

For those people who are struggling to pay a funeral bill or just need advice on what to do then 'Down to Earth' from Quaker Social Action provides excellent free, confidential, helpful, friendly organisational support. Based in London, they provide help to people all over the UK.

Visit: **https://quakersocialaction.org.uk/we-can-help/ helping-funerals/down-earth**

Telephone: 0208 983 5055

Cruse Bereavement

Cruse Bereavement Support provides a free helpful service, offering advice and empathy for people finding it hard to deal with the shock of bereavement and grief. Many people suffering from grief are unaware of the effect it can have on their health, both mental and physical.

Visit: **www.cruse.org.uk**

Freephone: 0808 808 1677

Samaritans

For anybody who may be bereaved by suicide and or feeling desperate or suicidal as a result of bereavement then the Samaritans are there to offer free advice 24/7.

Visit: **www.samaritans.org**

Freephone 24/7: 116 123

Sands

The Sands is a leading stillbirth/baby death UK charity. All bereavement support information is confidential. This charity aims to raise awareness of baby deaths and works with the government and other organisations to reduce the number of babies dying. They have a UK wide network of support groups, an online forum for families to connect together, as well as a bereavement support app.

Visit: **www.sands.org.uk/about-sands**
Freephone: 0808 164 3332

Death Certificates

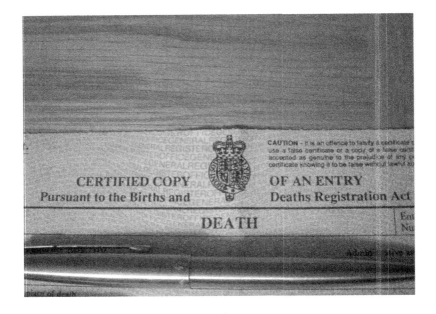

Once you have the medical certificate
www.bereavementadvice.org/topics/death-certificate-and-coroners-inquest/when-a-coroner-is-not-involved from a doctor or other paperwork from a Coroner (Procurator Fiscal in Scotland), you are then able to proceed with obtaining a death certificate and organise the funeral.

Obtaining a death certificate form online or in person at a registry office is one of the first and most important actions you can carry out. A death should be registered within five days (eight days in Scotland) at a registry office local to the deceased. The five or eight days include weekends and bank holidays. You will receive a certificate and a green form for burial or cremation. This form is handed into the cemetery or crematorium office before or at the funeral.

Why is a death certificate required?

A death certificate is an official document that serves as proof of a person's death. It contains important information about the deceased individual, such as their name, date of birth, date of death, cause of death, and location of death.

There are various reasons why a death certificate is required. Firstly, it provides legal proof of death, which is necessary for settling the deceased's estate, claiming life insurance, and other financial matters. Secondly, it helps to track mortality statistics, which can inform public health policies and initiatives. It also serves as a vital record that can be used for genealogical research and family history.

A death certificate is an essential document that provides important information about a person's passing and plays an important role in legal, financial, and administrative matters.

What is on a death certificate?

- The full name of the deceased person
- The date and place of death, including the time of death if known
- The cause of death, usually determined by a doctor or coroner
- The deceased person's date and place of birth
- The deceased person's occupation and usual address

- The name and address of the person who registered the death
- The date and place of the registration of the death
- The signature, name, and position of the registrar who registered the death
- The deceased person's marital status and the name of their spouse (if applicable)
- Any other information that may be relevant, i.e., the nationality or religion

Application links for a death certificate **online** are below – commonly searched as death certificate order.

England & Wales:
www.gov.uk/order-copy-birth-death-marriage-certificate
Scotland:
www.nrscotland.gov.uk/registration/how-to-order-an-official-extract-from-the-registers
Northern Ireland:
www.nidirect.gov.uk/services/order-death-certificate-online

Registry office application for a death certificate

If you prefer to visit the registry office, it is best to telephone them to inquire what paperwork you will need to bring. Although you will generally need to bring the following documents to provide evidence of the deceased:

- Occupation
- Date of birth
- Place of birth
- Address

If the deceased is a female who was married, you will also have to provide her husband (or late husband) name and occupation.

You will also need to provide evidence of your name and address as the person who is registering the death.

The Government operates a Tell Us Once **www.gov.uk/after-a-death/organisations-you-need-to-contact-and-tell-us-once** service which may save you time in submitting various information.

You can find your **local** registry office by following the links:

England & Wales:
www.gov.uk/register-offices
Scotland:
www.nrscotland.gov.uk/registration
Northern Ireland:
www.nidirect.gov.uk/contacts/district-registrars-northern-ireland

Extra copies of the death certificate may be needed to supply to organisations such as below:

- Banks and building societies
- Solicitors
- Pensions administrators
- Will executors or estate administrators
- Utility companies
- Insurance companies
- Local authority

Coroner's office

A coroner's office **www.judiciary.uk/courts-and-tribunals/ coroners-courts/coroners-appointments-contacts-and-area s/the-appointment-of-senior-coroners** is responsible for investigating deaths that occur under unusual or suspicious circumstances. The specific duties of a coroner's office can vary depending on the jurisdiction, but generally include the following:

- <u>Determining the cause and manner of death</u> The coroner's office investigates the circumstances surrounding a person's death, including any injuries or other evidence, in order to determine the cause and manner of death.
- <u>Identifying the deceased</u> The coroner's office works to identify the deceased, sometimes using fingerprints, dental records, or DNA testing.
- <u>Notifying next of kin</u> The coroner's office is responsible for notifying the deceased's next of kin and providing information about the death.
- <u>Collecting evidence</u> The coroner's office collects and preserves any evidence related to the death, including medical records, witness statements, and physical evidence.
- <u>Testifying in court</u> The coroner or a member of their staff may be called to testify in court about their investigation and findings related to the death.

Overall, the role of the coroner's office is to provide information to help determine the cause and manner of death and to ensure that justice is served in cases where foul play is suspected.

Death certificates from the coroner

If the local coroner's office is in England, Wales or Northern Ireland, the coroner's document for burial or cremation is called a "Coroner's Order for Burial" or "Coroner's Order for Cremation." In Scotland, the document is called a "Procurator Fiscal's Burial Order" or "Procurator Fiscal's Cremation Order." This document is issued to the funeral director handling the funeral arrangements and permits them to proceed with the burial or cremation.

If a post-mortem examination is required, the coroner may issue an "Interim Death Certificate", which is free of cost. This certificate allows the family to proceed with funeral arrangements and other administrative matters, such as applying for probate. However, the full death certificate will not be released until the coroner's inquiry has ended.

Once the coroner's inquiry has finished, the next of kin can register the death to obtain the full death certificate, which provides information about the cause of death and other relevant details.

In England, there is a charge for a doctor's signature on the medical certificate.

In Scotland, there is no charge for the two doctors' signatures on the certificate Form 5.

In Northern Ireland, there is no charge for one doctor's signature on Form B.

There is no charge in Wales, instead, a certificate known as Form E is issued by a Medical Referee.

However, in Wales, there are certain circumstances where a doctor's signature on a medical certificate may be required, and payable. For example, if the death occurred outside of Wales or if the cause of death is uncertain, a doctor's signature may be necessary to confirm the cause of death.

It's best to check with the undertaker or local registry office. Doctor's fees are not required to get a medical certificate for burial.

Whether you search for a death certificate online or in person at a registry office, ensure that you follow the law and obtain the certificate within the time frame of five days for England and eight days for Scotland.

For further help following a bereavement visit **savefuneralcosts.co.uk/support-with-bereavement/** for help and links to leading organisations.

Funeral Disbursements

When paying for funeral expenses undertakers may list their funerals as an all-inclusive (package) cost, or plus extra costs, these extra costs are called disbursements. These costs are incurred by a funeral director on behalf of the bereaved family, and are typically separate from the professional fees charged by the funeral director. Always ensure that you clearly understand a stated price includes these, or there will be additional disbursement costs, such as embalming and cremation/burial plot fees etc.

Funeral disbursements can include a wide range of costs when it comes to paying for funeral expenses. They may vary depending on the specific needs of the family and the requirements of the funeral service. Some common examples of funeral disbursements are shown below.

General disbursements

a) <u>Cremation fees</u> Can alter between different boroughs.

b) <u>Burial plot fees</u> Can alter enormously between different cemeteries especially in London and other cities.

c) <u>Cremation certificate</u> One doctor certificate.

d) <u>Funeral service</u> Spokesperson to conduct the service.

e) <u>Funeral service</u> Printed order of service sheet or booklet.

f) <u>Flowers</u> Flowers are a common feature of funeral services, and the cost of floral arrangements can vary depending on the size and type of arrangements.

g) <u>Embalming fee</u> This is needed after a post-mortem, and in other cases.

h) <u>Transport</u> Such as a limousine to transport family and mourners to the service.

i) <u>Transport of the deceased</u> Removal of the deceased from a nursing home or private residence out of office hours.

j) <u>Viewing the deceased</u> Charges for viewing the deceased out of office hours.

k) <u>Returned ashes</u> Cremated remains delivered to the family.

l) <u>Medical device removal</u> Removal of a pacemaker or other medical device for cremation.

m) <u>Oversized coffin</u> If the deceased was obese or very tall.

n) <u>Headstones</u> If the family wish to have a headstone erected.

o) <u>Newspaper notices</u> Families may wish to place notices in local newspapers to inform friends and acquaintances of the funeral service.

p) <u>Catering/Venue hire</u> It is common for families to hold a wake and provide food and refreshments for mourners following the funeral service.

q) <u>Religious or ceremonies</u> If the family wishes to incorporate specific religious or cultural traditions/ rituals into the funeral service.

r) <u>Music and entertainment</u> The family may wish to have music or other entertainment at the funeral service.

Saving on disbursements

When it comes to paying for funeral expenses, certain disbursements could be avoided as listed below:

a) If you arranged an early morning cremation, the fee can be reduced. If you have a cremation on a weekend, then the costs can double from the weekdays. The undertaker fees are also often increased for a weekend.
b) Inquire which are the cheaper cemeteries or natural burial sites.
d) If you arrange your own spokesperson.
e) Print your own order of service sheets/stapled booklet.
f) If you order the flowers directly from the florist, and not through an undertaker. Alternatively, if possible, you can use flowers from your garden.

g) Sometimes embalming is not necessary unless a post-mortem has been carried out. It is best to seek the advice of the undertaker to see if embalming is required.

h) If you inform your family members and guests to meet at the crematorium or cemetery, then you could cut out the cost of limousines.

j) If there are plans to see the deceased at an undertaker, try and visit during office hours.

k) If you were to have the ashes scattered on the crematorium gardens and not returned.

m) Purchase the coffin directly from a manufacturer (page 19).

n) Deal directly with a supplier of lower cost headstones.

o) Contact the newspaper yourself.

p) Organise the wake yourself.

q) Organise any ceremonies yourself.

r) Organise any music or entertainment yourself.

Paying for funeral expenses

Overall, paying for funeral expenses such as disbursements can add up to a significant cost of a funeral. However, an undertaker should help the family to ensure that the service is tailored to meet the specific needs and preferences of the family.

Funeral disbursements are separate from any government grants or benefits that may be available to the family of the deceased. For example, some families may be eligible for a bereavement payment to help cover funeral costs. Funeral directors may be able to provide guidance on any available financial assistance that may be available to the family.

Funeral disbursements are a necessary part of the funeral planning process, and people should be aware of the potential costs associated with a funeral service.

A brief history of funeral disbursements

The history of funeral disbursements can be traced back to ancient times when burial practices were an integral part of many cultures.

In ancient Egypt, the wealthy were buried in elaborate tombs that were filled with treasures, while the poor were buried in simple graves. Funeral expenses were paid by the family of the deceased and were seen as an important part of honouring the dead.

In ancient Greece, funeral rites were performed by family members and close friends, who were responsible for preparing the body for burial and arranging for the funeral procession. Funeral expenses were also paid by the family, and the cost of the funeral was often seen as an indication of the deceased's social status.

During the Middle Ages in Europe, funeral expenses were typically paid by the church or the local community. Funeral rites were often elaborate and included a procession through the streets, followed by a mass or other religious ceremony.

In modern times, funeral disbursements are typically paid for by the family of the deceased, or by their estate if they have made prior arrangements.

Cremations & Burials

Cremation fees vary from borough to borough, however direct cremation still remains the cheapest cremation. Statistics from Yougov **www.yougov.co.uk/topics/lifestyle/articles-reports/2016/08/16/majority-people-want-be-cremated-when-they-die** show that around 60% of people prefer cremation. The often high cost of the burial ground in a cemetery is one of the reasons cremations continue to rise in popularity. Natural burials have become more popular and provide an often cheaper burial cost in rural surroundings.

Choosing a crematorium

If you are working within a tight budget and your chosen undertaker has listed the cremation fee as a disbursement, you could inquire if a cremation would be less at another nearby crematorium, providing dates were still suitable.

However, if the same undertaker has an all-in cost (a package), you would be limited in choice, as most packages have a set crematorium. Many cremations are cheaper in the morning and on weekdays, afternoons and weekends are normally more expensive. Cremation fees can be quite heavily reduced in the early morning.

Direct Cremation

Why choose direct cremation?

Direct cremation does not involve a funeral service beforehand. Instead, this cremation service happens immediately, at the date/time agreed by the crematorium, without mourners. Over more recent years these have become far more popular, one of the reasons is that they are often the cheapest cremation.

After completing this process, the cremated ashes are returned to the family or dispersed at the crematorium garden. Having the ashes delivered to the family often incur extra charges.

Many people choose a simple funeral via a direct cremation funeral plan because they don't want to have the relatives left with the responsibility of sorting a funeral and reception. For others this cremation option is often for financial reasons, as direct cremations are cheaper and emotional reasons as this type of funeral is far easier to arrange.

Direct cremation is also a more environmentally-friendly option than traditional burials. Burials can have a negative impact on the environment due to the use of embalming chemicals, coffins and the space needed for burial plots and headstones. Cremation, on the other hand, uses far fewer resources and takes up much less space. Additionally, some crematoriums offer eco-friendly options, such as using biodegradable urns or planting trees in memory of the deceased.

As there are no mourners present at a direct cremation there are additionally no:

- Limousines to take family and mourners to the service
- Flowers
- Spokesperson required to read the service

- Order of service sheets for the service
- Organisation or stress to arrange the funeral
- Wake to organise
- Having to wear or hire suitable clothing such as a suit

Many families decide to conduct a celebration of life or memorial service for the beloved one after receiving the ashes. Due to the money saved with a direct cremation more money can often be put aside for a memorial service.

Council vs privately-run crematorium

For a full list of UK crematoriums visit.
www.cremation.org.uk/content/files/Crematoria%20by%20year%20of%20opening%2836%29.pdf

Council-run crematoriums are often significantly less expensive to use than privately-run crematoriums as they are operated on a not-for-profit basis. Additionally, council-run crematoriums may offer lower fees for local residents.

The main difference between council-run and privately-run crematoriums is the ownership and management of the facility. Council-run crematoriums are owned and operated by local government authorities, whereas privately-run crematoriums are owned and operated by private companies.

Another difference is the level of flexibility offered to families. Council-run crematoriums may have stricter policies and procedures in place, as they are governed by local government regulations. In contrast, privately-run crematoriums may have more flexibility when it comes to scheduling and personalising memorial services, as they are not bound by the same regulations.

Radiotherapy and cremation

Some articles suggest deceased people who have previously had radiotherapy treatment can pose a health risk when cremated as the cremation process can send radioactive particles into the air. However, at present deceased people who have undergone radiotherapy which is primarily used to treat cancer can be cremated.

To read more on finding affordable cremation services visit.

savefuneralcosts.co.uk/discover-cremations-near-me/

Burial ground

For a full list of UK_cemeteries visit.

**https://historicengland.org.uk/images-books/
publications/list-of-registered-cemeteries/registered-
cemeteries-list-jan18**

The cheapest possible burial ground can often be found by shopping around between different boroughs. The cost of burial plots can vary enormously from area to area. You can save a considerable amount of money by asking the undertaker how much a cemetery plot costs compared to others. Alternatively, you could look online at the cemeteries in different councils. Discounts for burials within the same borough where the deceased lived are often available.

Burial location

Although a local burial ground may cost more, many people choose a nearby cemetery or crematorium as that may have been the wish of the deceased or a place that is easy to visit. The location of the final resting place can be significant for many people, as it provides a place for them to visit and pay their respects. It can also bring comfort and closure to the bereaved to have their loved one buried in a familiar place close to home.

Ultimately, the decision on the burial ground is a personal one and should be made based on the wishes and needs of the deceased and their family.

Funeral Packages

Most low-cost undertakers offer different lower price funeral services which are often sold as funeral packages. Sometimes the costs are not fixed but plus disbursements. To help save funeral costs, you'll want to look at as many options as possible.

The three main questions about funeral packages are:

- What is included?
- Do you need everything?
- How does this funeral service compare to non-package funerals?

What are funeral packages?

Undertakers typically bundle together a range of funeral services, such as the cost of the coffin, care of the deceased, transportation, embalming, and other funeral-related expenses. By bundling these services together as a package, undertakers can offer a lower overall price instead of each service purchased separately.

Are funeral packages worth the money?

This is a matter of opinion, but there are certainly some good and bad points that you will want to consider. It's sensible to carefully read the details of the funeral package and compare it to the individual costs of each service. Undertakers may include services in the package which are not required for your needs. These services could end up increasing the overall cost of the funeral. For example, if you wanted to change the coffin for one that you may have purchased and decorated, it may not be possible to deduct the cost of the coffin in the package as it is part of the package.

Additionally, a funeral package may not include all the costs (disbursements) associated with a funeral, such as burial plot fees, obituary notices or order of service booklets. You should be aware of these additional costs and take them into consideration. It's important to compare prices and ask questions to ensure the package meets your needs and budget.

Benefits of funeral services in a package

- <u>Cost savings</u> They often offer a discounted price compared to purchasing each service separately. This can help families save money during a difficult time.
- <u>Convenience</u> They include a range of services that are needed for a funeral, such as transportation, organisation, and facilities. This can make the process more convenient for families.
- <u>Peace of mind</u> They can provide peace of mind for families, knowing that all necessary services are included and that the funeral will be handled by professionals.
- <u>Professional guidance</u> The services of a funeral director can provide guidance and support to families throughout the planning process.
- <u>Transparency</u> Funeral packages typically provide a clear breakdown of the costs involved, so families can understand exactly what they are paying for and avoid unexpected expenses.
- <u>Lower cost</u> Funeral packages can cost less money than arranging for all of the various elements of the funeral separately.

Disadvantages of funeral packages

Some people feel they have not had as much control over the funeral plans as they would have liked. With many packages you will have fewer options on things such as your choice of coffin, location and time of service. There may also be elements in the package that you do not need or want. Similarly, you might find that the funeral doesn't flow with the same level of personalisation as you would like. This lack of personalisation could leave you feeling upset and frustrated and are important points to consider.

Funeral services as a package

Funeral packages can provide families with a range of funeral services that can help ease the burden of planning a funeral and provide a meaningful farewell for their loved one.

They can also be one of the cheapest ways to include different funeral services, if you are happy with everything in the package. You could look into different cheap funeral packages when searching online for funeral directors near me. You would be more likely to save money this way.

Funeral Plans

When you're searching online for cheap funeral plans you want to know that you're getting the best possible deal and service for yourself or your loved one. In general, anyone over 18 can take out a funeral plan, although some companies restrict the age to over 50 and under 80.

The main selling point of a plan is that the cost is fixed; so that if for example you were to die twenty years after taking the plan out, your next of kin would not have to pay any extra costs. However, not all plans cover burial (plot fees) and cremation fees. These third-party costs can increase significantly over the years, so it's important to see if your plan does cover these fees.

Paying for a plan over many years is often not a good idea as you are normally charged interest. However, the exception to this is if you were to die within two years of paying for the plan. In this case the plan provider has to offer a full refund.

Since the 29th July 2022 funeral plan providers have to be regulated by the Financial Conduct Authority (FCA). **www.fca.org.uk/consumers/funeral-plans-check-provider-authorised** This also means that intermediaries such as funeral directors can no longer receive commission payments for selling funeral plans.

If you are going to buy a funeral plan check the Financial Services Register (FSR) **https://register.fca.org.uk/s** if the plan provider is listed and has permission to 'enter into a funeral plan contract'. This can be found in the section 'what can this firm do in the UK'.

If it is not on the list, it could be a representative of the plan provider. If this happens, find out who the plan provider is, and check that they are registered on the FSR. You could find out who is the plan provider by asking the company selling the plan.

If you need to complain about a plan provider, contact the Financial Ombudsman Service (FOS). **www.financial-ombudsman.org.uk**.

Key points when comparing different plans

A funeral plan is generally worth taking out if

- You do not have to borrow money to take the plan out - You can pay the fees without any interest (if paying by instalments).
- You want to be cremated – Most plans include cremation fees. Your next of kin or family would find it difficult to deal with sorting out a funeral and likewise paying for one. Either they would not have enough money, or you would not have left enough to cover the cost of a funeral.

It's generally not worth taking out a funeral plan if

- You intend to move area – Most plans will allow you to move, however, may have to pay increased fees with a new undertaker local to where you are moving.
- If you have to get into debt to pay for the plan – Avoid debt wherever you can.
- You intend to move abroad – The plan will not cover you.
- The plan repayments are over many years which include interest payments – The total cost may outweigh what the plan is worth.

What is generally included

- Transporting and caring for the deceased.
- Visiting the deceased in a chapel of rest.
- Coffin and funeral director fees.
- Hearse to transport the coffin to the service.
- An allowance towards or all of the cremation fees.

What is not generally included

- Burial plot fees – These can be literally thousands, so it's important to make inquiries and check different council burial fees
- Church service
- Headstones and memorials
  savefuneralcosts.co.uk/price-of-a-headstone/
- Order of service booklets
- Flowers
  savefuneralcosts.co.uk/funeral-flower-ideas/
- Catering for a wake (page 28)

Fees which often vary between being included or not

- Spokesperson to read the service
- Embalming
- Limousines for mourners
- Doctors fee of £82 for cremations – Not applicable in Scotland

Possible restriction

- The day and time of day for the funeral

It is very important to see what is covered and what is not covered when comparing costs. For example, one provider may seem cheaper as their advertised cost may start at a lower level than others, but then say plus additional services. When these extra services are added on, they may total more than another plan provider for a like-for-like service.

The other thing to bear in mind is that some plan providers may be cheaper at offering a cremation, but their burial service may be significantly higher than others.

Plan with Grace (PWG) **www.planwithgrace.co.uk** offers both cremation and burial funeral plans. Their aim is to provide clients with quality low-price local funeral plans in the UK.

In common with some other providers PWG offers:

- Guaranteed acceptance
- No medicals
- Pay-in-full
- Monthly payment funeral plans

For example, PWG 'Tulip' cremation service includes, nationwide collection, dressing of deceased in chosen clothes, family support & guidance, choice of day and time of service, undertaking fees, hearse, bearers, spokesperson fees, doctors' fees, cremation fees, and return of ashes as standard.

PWG also offers a free will service when you take out a plan. When taking out a free will service it is important to check that it is not a condition of the free will that you have to use the chosen solicitor as an executor of the will. This would mean that the solicitor would charge for all work as an executor carrying out the wishes of the deceased. Normally a family member is appointed as an executor.

In the UK, writing a will can be carried out by anyone who is over 18 years old and is of sound mind. However, a will must be written correctly to be legally binding. Solicitors are qualified legal professionals who can provide expert advice on wills and estates. If no will is left then probate has to be applied.

However, as plans and costs can change it is always a good idea before buying a plan to shop around and compare other leading plan providers such as:

Golden Charter Funeral Plans – Standard Plan
www.goldencharter.co.uk/funeral-plans/standard-plan

Avalon Funeral Plans – Standard Funeral Plan
**www.avalonfuneralplans.com/uk-funeral-plans/standard
-funeral-plan/**

For example, Golden Charter offers burial or cremation on their Standard Plan. If you were thinking of burial this may work out cheaper than other plans, depending on what you would like included.

Important points for a funeral plan

Check that your chosen plan provider is listed on the FSR and provides national coverage.

Searching for funeral plans can be overwhelming. Inquire if the plan provider uses local undertakers relative to each area, as this is often best for the customer.

Additionally, check if a provider can offer easier payments by arranging monthly instalments. PWG for example, offers up to two years interest free, or a one-off payment. PWG instalment payments between three and five years are presently charged at 6.5% interest.

Writing a Will

Writing a will is an important step in ensuring that your wishes are respected, and your loved ones are provided for after your death. Despite this, many people neglect to write a will, either because they believe they do not have enough assets to make it worthwhile, they cannot be bothered, think it's a waste of money, or because they simply do not want to confront the idea of their own mortality.

However, the reality is that failing to write a will can lead to a range of problems and complications for your loved ones after you're gone. If you die without a will, and there is no other living relatives your estate will be subject to the law of intestacy, **www.gov.uk/inherits-someone-dies-without-will** which have different rules in different areas such as, England and Wales, Scotland, Northern Ireland, and outside of the UK.

This means that your assets will be distributed according to a set of legal rules, rather than your wishes. This can lead to disputes, stress and tension among family members, at an already emotional time. Following legal rules may well not reflect your true intentions.

No will = no control

In addition, without a will, you will have no control over who will manage your estate after you're gone. This means that the court will appoint an administrator to manage your affairs, rather than an executor who you could have chosen and trust to carry out your wishes. This can lead to delays, complications, and potentially even mistakes, as the administrator may not have the necessary skills or knowledge to manage your estate effectively. Likewise, if a solicitor is appointed as an executor, their often-heavy fees will be deducted from the estate. This obviously leaves less money for the relatives.

A will can also help to minimise the amount of inheritance tax **www.gov.uk/valuing-estate-of-someone-who-died** that your estate will have to pay. The will can be structured in a way that takes advantage of tax exemptions and reliefs, helping to ensure that more of your assets go to your loved ones rather than to the taxman.

Perhaps most importantly, writing a will provides peace of mind for both you and your loved ones. It ensures that your wishes are respected and that your loved ones are provided for in the way that you would have wanted. It can also help to avoid disputes and tensions among family members, as everyone knows exactly what your wishes are and how your estate will be distributed.

Who can write a will

In the UK, a will can be written by anyone who is over 18 years old and is of sound mind. While solicitors are qualified legal professionals who can provide expert advice on wills and estates, they are not the only ones who can write a will on behalf of a client.

If you are writing your will, you must sign it in front of two witnesses, who must also sign it. Importantly you cannot leave witnesses or their spouses anything in your will. Witnesses do not have to sign the will at the same time as each other. Apart from signing the witnesses must also write name, address and occupation. If at a later date you wish to change the will (known as a 'Codicil' – official alteration) then you must repeat the same witnesses and signature procedure. If, however you decide to make a completely new will, then the old will must be destroyed and made clear in the new will that any previous wills are revoked.

Writing a will for free

Writing a will for free is popular and many individuals choose to write their own wills using low-cost DIY will kits **www.lawpack .co.uk/wills/wills?order=OrderByPriceDESC** or low-cost online will-writing. **https://farewill.com/make-a-will-online**. However, it is important to point out that will writing is NOT regulated unless using a solicitor.

Regulations for will writing

To ensure that the process of writing a will is carried out correctly, being valid and legally binding, and that it accurately reflects the individual's wishes, many people choose to seek the assistance of a solicitor or other qualified professional when writing their will. As solicitors are regulated you are covered by many important regulations.

Examples when very advisable to use professional services:

- Your normal residence is abroad
- You have property abroad
- You own a business
- Other family members who may make a claim on your will, such as a second spouse or children from a previous relationship
- You share a property with someone who is not your spouse or civil partner
- You wish to give money or assets to a dependant who is unable to look after themselves

It's important to note that if a will is not written correctly, it may not be legally valid, and this can cause complications for the individual's estate and their loved ones after they pass away. Therefore, it is recommended to seek professional advice when writing a will to ensure that it is accurate, valid, and legally binding.

Key points for writing a will

There are several reasons why it is important to write a will. Here are some of the key points:

- Control over distribution of assets Writing a will allows you to decide how your assets, such as money, property, and possessions, will be distributed after your death. This ensures that your wishes are granted and that your loved ones are provided for.

- <u>Protection of family members</u> If you have dependents, such as children or elderly relatives, a will can provide for their care and support after your death. For example, you can appoint a guardian for your children, or leave a specific sum of money for the care of an elderly relative.
- <u>Avoiding disputes</u> Without a will, your assets will be distributed according to the laws of intestacy, which may not reflect your wishes or the needs of your loved ones. This can lead to disputes and legal challenges from family members, which can be time-consuming and costly.
- <u>Appointing an executor</u> A will allows you to appoint an executor to manage your estate after your death. This ensures that your estate is managed by someone you trust, and who has the necessary skills and knowledge to handle your affairs.
- <u>Tax planning</u> Writing a will can also help you to minimise the amount of inheritance tax that your estate will have to pay. A solicitor or other qualified professional can provide advice on how to structure your will to minimise tax liabilities.

Making a will

The Government website sets out the basic information of making a will in England **www.gov.uk/make-will**

There are different regulations in Scotland for will writing **www.citizensadvice.org.uk/scotland/family/death-and-will s/wills-s/** and Northern Ireland **www.nidirect.gov.uk/articles/making-will**

Bear in mind that if you choose to use a solicitor to be the executor of your will, that solicitor's fees can be high and may even be based on a percentage of the total value of your estate. It is for this reason that many people choose a family member to be an executor.

Updating your will

Things in life move on quickly and for many things often change. Therefore, after writing a will it's important to think of updating your will every few years if things change such as:

- Moving property
- Having children
- Getting married as this will revoke any previous wills
- Getting separated or divorced

What is probate?

In brief, applying for probate **www.gov.uk/applying-for-probate** is a legal right to deal with someone's estate, when they die. You should therefore not put any property on the sale market or make other financial plans until probate has been granted.

No will - Is probate needed?

Yes, probate would be needed if a person dies without writing a will as their estate will be subject to the law of intestacy. This means that the nearest living relative can apply for probate with no will. **www.gov.uk/applying-for-probate/if-theres-not-a-a-will**.

The process of administering the estate and distributing the assets is managed by the Probate Court, and the person responsible for managing the process is called the

Administrator, rather than the Executor (who would be appointed by a will).

There are different probate rules in Scotland **www.scotcourts. gov.uk/taking-action/dealing-with-a-deceased%27s-estate -in-scotland** where it is referred to as Confirmation, and different probate rules in Northern Ireland. **www.nidirect.gov.uk/articles/probate**.

Farewill the low-cost probate specialists offer low-cost probate services **https://farewill.com/apply-for-probate**.

Taking action on will writing

Writing a will for free, or through a qualified person is an important step in ensuring that your wishes are respected, your loved ones are provided for, and your estate is managed in the way that you would have wanted after your death. If you have not yet written a will, it is never too late to get started. If you do not feel you are able to write a will then speak to a solicitor or other qualified professional for advice.

Storing a will

It is important to store the will in a safe place and make any executors aware of where it is stored. Apart from storing in a safe place at home, such as a fireproof safe, both banks and solicitors can provide safe storage.

Funeral Directory

Please note:

All information and costs are correct March 2023.

Please telephone or visit the links to confirm up to date information and costs.

Funeral directors normally charge extra if the deceased was bariatric (obese) or very tall as the coffin would have to be a non-standard larger coffin. Additional charges are often made for out of hours/area collection, embalming, and pacemaker/ device removal before cremation.

Listed below in the funeral directory are contact details for services & suppliers in Steps 1-5 including additional cremation ash jewellery, diamond and glass flower creators.

- Low-cost independent undertakers based in South England
- National low-cost undertakers
- Regional low-cost independent undertakers
- Northern Ireland for Direct Cremation
- To book a Salvation Army officer
- To book a Humanist
- To book a Celebrant
- Coffin suppliers
- Van transport service
- Biodegradable urns
- The Natural Death Centre
- Grave digging service
- Funeral plans
- The Environment Agency
- Garden Stones/Headstones & Memorials
- Dried flower wreaths
- Jewellery from cremation ashes
- Diamonds from cremation ashes
- Ashes in glass flowers

Low-cost independent undertakers based in South England

South East England/Nationwide for Cremations & Burials

TDM Funeral Services – A direct cremation from £1200 including collection of ashes. A simple cremation is from £1941. TDM are proud to assist low-income families or those on benefits. Other attended cremation packages and burials are also available. Funerals outside of the South East may incur additional fees.

Fieldings
Stoneheap Road
East Studdal
Dover
Kent
CT15 5BU
Freephone: 01304 356616

www.tdmfunerals.co.uk

They can also add special services to fully personalise a funeral.

- Dove or balloon release
- Specially-created memorial video
- Order of service sheets
- Musical tributes, such as bands or choirs
- A range of coffins and caskets
- Floral tribute hire
- Family limousine
- Motor, motorbike or horse-drawn hearse

South East England/Nationwide for Cremations & Burials

BB Funerals – A direct cremation from £895 + £100 return of ashes + £82 doctors fee (if applicable) + removal of a medical device, i.e. pacemaker (if applicable) + embalming (if applicable). A simple cremation funeral is from £1000 + disbursements. Other attended cremation packages and burials are also available. Funerals outside of the South East may incur additional fees.

16-18 Church Hill Road
Barnet

EN4 8TB
Telephone: 0208 441 6062
Mobile: 07538 276130

www.brooks-funerals-directors.co.uk

National low-cost undertakers

England/Isle of Wight/Isle of Man/Scotland & Islands/ Wales for Direct Cremations

The Funeral Market – A direct cremation service covering the entire UK (excluding Northern Ireland) and including the Scottish islands/Isle of Wight/Man from £999 including return of ashes + £82 doctors fee (if applicable) + removal of a medical device, i.e. pacemaker (if applicable) + embalming (if applicable) + ferry fee if travelling to the Scottish islands/Isle of Wight/Man. Other attended cremation packages are also available.

Brewery House
4 Castle Street
Buckingham
MK18 1BS
Freephone: 0800 689 1060

www.thefuneralmarket.com

England/Scotland/Wales for Direct Cremations

Farewill – A direct cremation service covering England/ mainland Scotland/Wales from £800 + £82 doctors fees (if applicable) + removal of a medical device, i.e. pacemaker (if applicable) + embalming (if applicable) + £150 for those wishing to have the ashes returned within five days, or £50 within thirty days.

Unit 1
27 Downham Road
London
N1 5AA
Telephone: 0208 138 0719

https://farewill.com/funerals/direct-cremation

England/Wales for Direct Cremation

Cremation Funeral – Covering England/Wales with a direct cremation for in most cases £795. Additional fees would be transportation of the deceased to a funeral director, doctor's certificate at £82 (if applicable) + removal of a medical device, i.e., pacemaker (if applicable) + oversize coffin (if applicable) + embalming (if applicable) + £90 for those wishing to have the ashes returned. At an additional expense the ashes can be couriered internationally if needed.

Kilbury Drive
Worcester
Worcestershire
WR5 2NE
Telephone: 01299 828771

www.cremationfuneral.co.uk

Regional low-cost independent undertakers

Listed below are additional low-cost undertakers who offer direct cremations & burials, and the areas they cover.

Hull and East Yorkshire for Cremation & Burials

Legacy Funerals - Covering East Yorkshire and Hull for cremations and burials. A direct cremation is from £970 and attended cremation from £1799 including a simple ashes container. Other attended cremation packages and burials are also available.

730 Anlaby Road
Hull
HU4 6BP
Telephone: 01482 562762

www.legacyfuneraldirectors.co.uk

Southern Scotland for Cremation & Burials

Mitchells Funerals – Covering a large area of southern Scotland with a direct cremation for £800 including the ashes returned around the Glasgow area. Additional fees for funeral and return of ashes outside of Glasgow area. Mitchells also offer a traditional cremation service from £1695, and a free funeral for 17 years old and under. Burials can also be arranged.

23a Stonelaw Road
Rutherglen
Glasgow
G73 3TW
Freephone: 0808 196 8657

www.mitchellsfunerals.co.uk

Mainland Scotland for Direct Cremation

Caledonia Cremation – A charity non-profit funeral director covering all mainland Scotland with a Direct Cremation. They also offer emotional support and practical advice on helping claiming funeral benefits for £1095 + £95 for those wishing to have the ashes returned. Additional services include helping a customer access services for ashes to be made into jewellery or fireworks.

18 Orkney Street
Glasgow
G51 2BX
Telephone: 03000 113311

www.caledoniacremation.org.uk

Northern Ireland for Direct Cremation

Pure Cremation – A direct cremation service operating in Northern Ireland Pure Cremation's Northern Ireland partner for £1295 if the deceased passed away in hospital, or £1445 if passed away at home. No fee for return of ashes.

117 Shankill Rd
Belfast
BT13 1FD
Telephone: 028 9600 9600

https://ni.purecremation.com

To book a Salvation Army officer

Salvation Army
101 Newington Causeway
London
SE1 6BN
Telephone: 0207 367 4500

www.salvationarmy.org

To book a Humanist

Humanists
39 Moreland Street
London
EC1V 8BB
Telephone: 0207 324 3060

www.humanism.org.uk

To book a Celebrant

Funeral Celebrant
PO Box 116
Barton Upon Humber
North Lincolnshire
DN18 9AL
Mobile: 07469 192644

www.independentcelebrants.com/find-a-celebrant

Coffin suppliers

If you are planning a natural burial always check with the natural burial site that the coffin you are thinking of purchasing is allowed. If the deceased has been embalmed, you should also check if this is accepted at a natural burial site.

Compare the Coffin
Freephone: 0800 690 6513

www.comparethecoffin.com

Feet First Coffins
11 Rycroft
Furzton
Milton Keynes
MK4 1AH
Telephone: 01908 506768
Mobile: 07971 600515

www.feetfirstcoffins.co.uk

Cardboard Coffin Company
Cameron Street
Cardiff
CF24 2NW
Telephone: 02920 098979

www.cardboardcoffincompany.com

Sussex Willow Coffins
11 Sussex Square
Brighton
BN2 5AA
Telephone: 07592 353845

www.sussexwillowcoffins.co.uk

Somerset Willow Coffins
The Wireworks Estate
Bristol Road
Bridgwater
Somerset
TA6 4AP
Telephone: 01278 424003

www.somersetwillowcoffins.co.uk

Green Coffin Company Ltd
Lynton
Guilsborough Hill
Hollowell
Northampton
NN6 8RN
Freephone: 0800 193 0353

www.thegreencoffincompany.co.uk

Van transport service

To transport the empty decorated coffin to the undertaker.

Anyvan
5th Floor
The Triangle
5-17 Hammersmith Grove
London
W6 0LG
Telephone: 0203 872 3050

www.anyvan.com

Biodegradable urns

For handmade bespoke biodegradable urns.

Biodegradable urns
Telephone: 01379 677344

www.eco-urns.co.uk

The Natural Death Centre

For a list of natural burial sites.

Natural Death Centre
In The Hill House
Watley Lane
Twyford
Winchester
SO21 1QX
Telephone: 01962 712690

www.naturaldeath.org.uk

Grave digging service

This service operates nationwide.

Graveworks
Unit 9
Dencora Park
18 Shire Hill
Saffron Walden
Essex
CB11 3GB
Telephone: 01799 521498

www.graveworks.co.uk

Funeral plans

For low-cost quality funeral plans.

Plan with Grace
35 Catherine Place
London
SW1E 6DY
Freephone: 0800 471 4689

www.planwithgrace.com/pre-paid-funeral-plans

The Environment Agency

For advice on home burial regulations.

National Customer Contact Centre
PO Box 544
Rotherham

S60 1BY
Telephone: 03708 506506

www.gov.uk/government/organisations/environment-agency

Garden Stones/Headstones & Memorials

Deal directly with one of the three monumental masons for Garden Stones/Headstones & Memorials.

Southern Memorials Ltd
Unit 11
Ropery Business Park
48 Anchor & Hope Lane
Charlton
London
SE7 7RX
Telephone: 0208 305 0238

www.southernmemorials.co.uk/home

Abbey Memorials
Rawreth Industrial Estate
Rawreth Lane
Rayleigh
Essex
SS6 9RL
Telephone: 01268 782757

www.abbeymemorialsltd.co.uk

Rustic Stone
The Old Fox
Fox Hill
Hollesley

Woodbridge
Suffolk
IP12 3RD
Telephone: 0844 811 1373

www.rusticstone.net/garden-memorial-stones

Dried flower wreaths

Beautiful, handmade, bespoke, lasting dried flower wreaths and arrangements.

Botanical Tales
East Devon

www.botanicaltales.com

Jewellery from cremation ashes

Jewellery from cremated ashes.

Hand on Heart
Unit 1
The North Range
Hackthorpe Hall Business Centre
Hackthorpe
Penrith
Cumbria
CA10 2HX

www.handonheartjewellery.co.uk/collections/cremation-ashes-jewellery

AlmaBlue
1952 S
La Cienega Blvd
Los Angeles
CA 90034
USA
Telephone: 001 858 208 6089

www.almablue.net

Diamonds from cremation ashes

Diamonds from cremated ashes.

Eterneva Diamonds
Austin
Texas
USA
Telephone: 001 512 766 5011

www.eterneva.com/loved-ones

Ashes in glass flowers

Bespoke glass flowers filled with ashes and sealed.

Ashes in Flowers
Stourbridge
West Midlands
Telephone: 07815 462275

www.ashesinflowers.uk

Printed in Great Britain
by Amazon